BIG PICTURE PRESS

First published in the UK in 2025 by Big Picture Press,
an imprint of Bonnier Books UK
5th Floor, HYLO, 105 Bunhill Row,
London, EC1Y 8LZ
The authorised representative in the EEA is
Bonnier Books UK (Ireland) Limited.
Registered office address:
Floor 3, Block 3, Miesian Plaza,
Dublin 2, D02 Y754, Ireland
compliance@bonnierbooks.ie

1 3 5 7 9 10 8 6 4 2

ISBN 978-1-80078-711-7

This book was typeset in Jungle Giant and Stupid Questions
The illustrations were created in gouache and watercolour

Bulldog clip: creativesunday – stock.adobe.com
Paperclip: natatravel – stock.adobe.com

Edited by Charlie Wilson and Josephine Southon
Designed by Jenny Hastings
Production by Giulia Caparrelli

Printed in Latvia

On the Streets of

PARIS

A poetic tour of the city

Clémentine Beauvais
Seula Yi

BPP

Take a Walk with Me

"As a Parisian, could you write a few poems about Paris?"
It's a trickier question than it sounds. I'm a Parisian who isn't
actually Parisian — I grew up there, but I left at eighteen to
begin a new life in a new country: the UK.

My family is still in Paris, and I visit often — neither a tourist
nor a Parisian, but somewhere in between. Luckily, in-between
places are the perfect places for poetry.

Many of these poems stem from memories of my childhood and
teenage years. When I was younger, I didn't always love Paris;
it felt too crowded. I longed for holidays, yearning to see the
countryside and the sea.

But there were moments of grace that made the dull, grey school year suddenly brighter. Sometimes, it was just a glimpse of the Eiffel Tower peeking out from behind a building, or walking along the Seine on warm summer nights — listening to music and feeling free, full of hope.

Paris, like most capital cities, has a rich history, filled with both joyful and difficult times. In this book, I wanted to show the city's many sides: the cheerful moments as well as the places where the past has left its marks.

Whether you are reading this in a Paris café or simply dreaming of visiting one day, I hope this book takes you on a poetic journey through the City of Light.

Clémentine Beauvais

Hello, Eiffel Tower

Hello, Eiffel Tower, here you are
poking out of that tree
peeking around the corner of that street
always playing hide-and-seek you are

never where I think you are
never where I expect to see you
never the size you should be
never the right angle. Tell me

how do you lift that steely 'A' of yours
so swiftly from nowhere to me,
when I wasn't thinking of you,
wasn't feeling playful. Till now.

Now I'm ready for another game
trickster tower jungle gym for clouds
tourist monkey puzzle cheeky queen
count to ten and you'll be gone again.

Baguette: The Rules

If you buy the baguette,
the rule is you get
to eat just a bit,
just the tip,
on the way home.

The rule is the baguette
will never make it home
with its head still on.
It would be wrong,
very wrong.

The rule is you walk
out of the bakery,
and whatever sticks out
of the warm paper sleeve
is yours to eat.

So break it,
and eat it.
It's yours.
You've earned it.

Gare du Nord

Thrumming with trains announcements whistles beeping
throngs of tourists travellers loiterers barterers
public piano players luggage luggers
speaking tongues faster than the softly slowing trains.
Most people leave the station quick, just transit.   *Not Paris,*
                                                                                not quite yet,
                                                                                tourists think.

But they are wrong: it *is*
Paris; not the Paris of bérets and baguettes,
but the Paris that brings to its own body,
through tentacles of railway lines,
its life: the people from outside its walls,
people who live in cities not called Paris.
Your trip may well start here, may well end here,
so remember: what welcomed you
was not stacks of choux in bakers' windows.
What welcomed you was a city, neither here nor there,
not quite sure what to do with its own history, which the yo-yoing trains
bring in and out each day so the city can run.

Welcome, get your fill of the noises, the voices,
the screeching brakes, the laughter, the twang
of the public piano player. As you step off the train, pay attention.
Mind the gap

between our real Paris

and the Paris of your imagination.

Café Life

Today I'm feeling extremely Parisian.
So I'd better show myself to the tourists.
I shall wear my chic things, and I shall take a book,
and I shall wear my nonchalant look.
I shall sip a small coffee at a café nearby,
en terrasse, with the wind in my face,
and I'll act like I'm part of the landscape.

Every detail must be right. The pigeons must coo.
The waiter must be rude, and my cheeks must be rouged,
and I'll stare at the book, and I'll stare at the sky,
and sometimes I'll sigh,
and I won't notice you taking photos of me,
        or talking about me,
        or thinking about me,
and I'll live on forever in your stories of Paris,
        spiky with upspeak:
"We saw this woman; she was, like, so chic?
She had, like, a book?
and a nonchalant look?
and she was sipping coffee?
at a café nearby?
Ah! Those Parisians, *un café, un livre,*
la joie de vivre."

It's tiring. It's a job. It's a duty. It's a mission,
that whole thing of being, sometimes, a Parisian.

Bouquinistes

A bottle-green tortoise treasure chest
kept by a windswept, street-sure bookseller,
propped against the parapet along the Seine;
its shell pops open at the first rays of sun.

It's called a bouquiniste 'cos there are books in it.
(Unofficial hypothesis. Don't quote me on it.)
And also prints, and Paris kit and trinkets. It's a bit like magic,
how it all fits in that box. There must be a trick.

My favourite things here are the very old books
wrapped in squeaky plastic, the price in felt-tip on it; I find it,
somehow,   touching, that care,
the care it took to wrap those books.

In fact, the only good reason
ever to write a book
is that maybe one day it will end up at a bouquiniste.
Wrapped in plastic, with the price in felt-tip on it.

Under Paris

There's another Paris under Paris,
beneath the skin, you'll find the veins:
metro lines, slim and green, then the thick RER
clanging through the arteries.

There's another Paris under Paris,
past the veins, you'll find the bowels:
miles of soupy sewers, tidily labelled
with street-name signs from the surface.

There's another Paris under Paris,
deeper than the bowels, the bones:
the Catacombs, cavefuls of skulls,
corridorfuls of flat-packed skeletons.

There's still more of Paris under Paris,
an ever-dark marrow: the buried river Bièvre.
That one you can't visit. It flows beneath, unseen.
Imagine it rumbling deep down under your feet.

Wallace Fountains

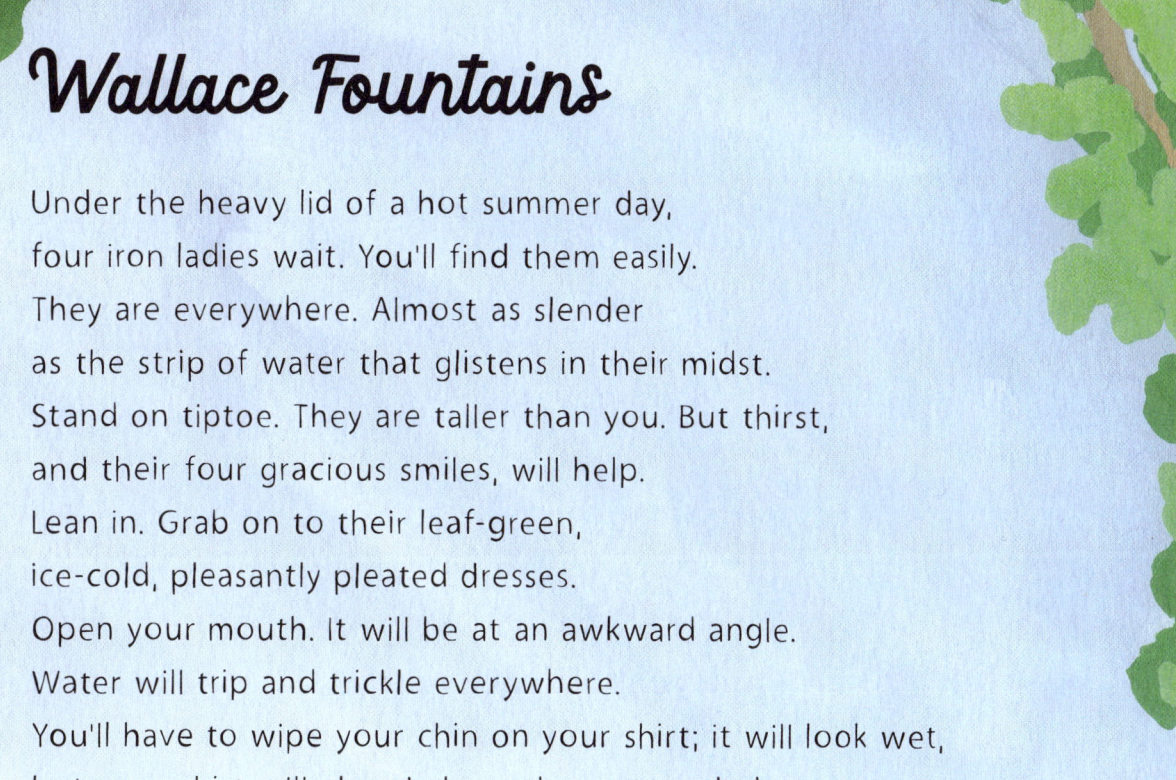

Under the heavy lid of a hot summer day,
four iron ladies wait. You'll find them easily.
They are everywhere. Almost as slender
as the strip of water that glistens in their midst.
Stand on tiptoe. They are taller than you. But thirst,
and their four gracious smiles, will help.
Lean in. Grab on to their leaf-green,
ice-cold, pleasantly pleated dresses.
Open your mouth. It will be at an awkward angle.
Water will trip and trickle everywhere.
You'll have to wipe your chin on your shirt; it will look wet,
but your shirt will already bear the wet en dash
of their wet pedestal against your bellyful
of water. That water tastes like it was given to you by somewhere else—

not the rusty pipes that run under Paris,
but the mountains, maybe. This water, I want to believe,
comes from glaciers directly.
Thank the ladies. Now your thirst is slaked,
your shirt is soaked, you are
ready to face the sun again.

Unknown Soldier at the Arc de Triomphe

Lying there for us all, he stands for them all,
and he stands for the lies that were told
when they took all the boys from their toys,
from their homes, boys from here, boys from there,
and the boys from abroad in the sun-splattered lands.
"Just a quick war," they said, and they buried them fast,
in the earth of the north
where the grass
can't grow back.

All the cars spin and spin round his small, sturdy flame,
his home is called Triumph, we will not know his name,
and I pass by his home with my own little boys,
who don't know, who don't care, and I think of those times
when they took all those boys from their toys, from their homes,
and they said it'd be fast. And I squeeze the small fists
of my sons in my hands. That's what staring at Triumph
does to you sometimes.

    He could be anyone,
he could be my grandfather, he could be my son,
the unknown soldier at the Arc de Triomphe,
where the heart of the city pumps its cars round and round.

21st June, Music Day

It's the shortest night of the year,
it's the longest night of the year:
21st June, Music Day.
Anyone can come out and play music that night,
right there, on the street.
A recent tradition. Started with 1980s kids scratching
guitars, watching people around begin to dance
in the bright evening sun till the end of the night and beyond,
well into 22nd June.

As children, we love it. Walking out with parents later than is allowed.
Parents softer than usual, their gazes vague, their bodies swaying,
and the night is so long when the sun is still out, with you, playing.

As teenagers, we love it. Parents are out with the younger siblings.
And we, in the warm sunlight of evening, might be doing anything,
like kissing, maybe, and eating kebabs
to the drum of a reggae band between four blocks.

As adults, we love it. It is oddly melancholy;
there is something in it that still smells like 1980s spirit,
and we know that the world is in no better shape,
but there's someone there playing,
all that matters is sound, is dance, is beat,
and listening to the midnight sun on the concrete.

The Louvre

I love this anecdote from long ago,
a real story, and one to make you... reflect.
Now shuffle yourself back to early last century.
Someone had decided that the Mona Lisa
was in need of better protection,
so the Musée du Louvre had it covered with glass.

Good glass.

Strong glass.

Reflective glass.

So people looked at her and only saw   themselves,
which they really didn't need a museum for.

One day, a guy called Roland Dorgelès,
who wins my heart as French history's biggest prankster,
armed with a razor blade, a brush and foam
and a sense of humour, walked into the museum,
planted himself in front of the Mona Lisa
and started shaving his moustache, very appreciative
of such a nicely framed mirror in such a lovely public space.
Apparently, the museum security
didn't find it funny.
But I do!

And I think of you, Roland Dorgelès,
when I struggle to spot the Mona Lisa
through the forest of handheld screens
reflecting people's faces alongside it.

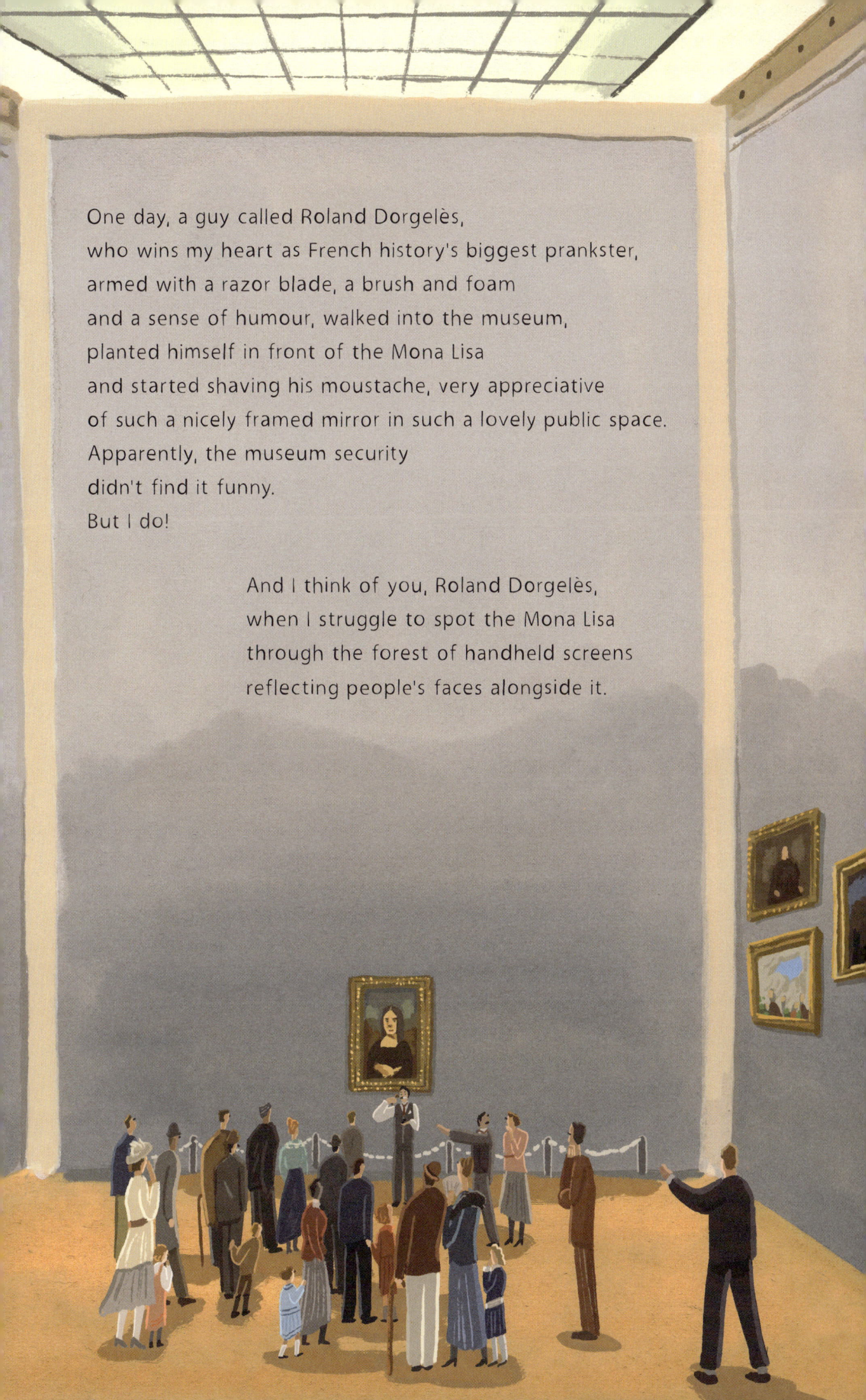

Montparnasse Cemetery

I used to do some of my homework there,
on a bench not too far from where Baudelaire is buried,
    the great poet,
     next to his stepfather, like a child,
and on his weirdly tiny tombstone, a snowfall
of notes left there by teenagers. *Love you Charles!*
                         Best poet ever!
I know Baudelaire hated his stepfather,
so I hope that the notes cheer him up.
This cemetery is full of teenagers from neighbouring schools,
full of shy side-glances, prompt to retract, like snails' eyestalks.
It is a place of first kisses, of cats, of shady trees. It is very tidy.
A lady fills up a watering can from a rusty tap,
and the pipe's slender body shakes, as if to say
that in the deep, deep earth, where the water comes from,
everything vibrates
with life.

Notre-Dame

Hail, Notre-Dame, full of flames,
hail of glass and stone, Notre-Dame, hallowed be thy name
that we whispered as we watched you with eyes made orange by fire,
black by smoke and white by terror.
The stone is so hot, they said on the radio,
that it could very well start melting.
And we were turned to stone,
as your own stone turned soft.
That night, we swapped skins.
We watched as the spindle rising from your spine
                              collapsed
                                into
                                you
                    like our hearts into our bellies.

Hail, Mary, full of bells.
We were there when they set up that friendly yellow crane,
as they fixed your tortoise shell at tortoise speed.
You did get fixed, and in the end it felt like it was quick.
We were there, a crowd of smiles, when, for the very first time,
we heard your bell again. The beating of your heart,
slotted right back where it belonged.   Healed!
Though ever since the fire, the peal of your bell
has been ringing, let's say,   orange, just a tinge,
just as if, deep inside you, one stone were still burning.

The Green Highway

Instead of a train, a park.
Instead of curtains, wisteria.
Instead of passengers, passers-by.
Instead of a driver, a dog.
Instead of tickets, sunglasses.
Instead of a clock, a dandelion.
Instead of luggage, a pocket.
Instead of steam, sparrows.
Instead of crosswords, butterflies.
Instead of speed, a stroll.
Instead of rails, a path.

La Galerie des Glaces

So in French, 'glace' means *mirror* and also *ice cream*,
and in Versailles, the palace of former kings and queens,
there is a hall of mirrors.   Guess what it's called.

Now guess what all French kids think it's about
as their parents wake them up one Saturday morning
                              when they'd rather sleep in
and say, "We're going to Versailles, the home of the Sun King,
blah blah blah history, blah blah blah France's past glory."
The flowerbeds so close-clipped they don't dare shed a petal,
the salons so golden your eyelashes will tingle,
the chapel that's carved in the preciousest stones,
                    and then, the final thing,
at the end, the best thing: *La Galerie des Glaces.*

So of course we tagged along, all the little French children,
we glanced at the fountains, the salons, the gardens,
                                        and when at long last
we reached the final thing,   *La Galerie des Glaces*
we saw that it was   just a hall of mirrors.
It's the largest hall of mirrors in the entire world.
It is full of French children with the most puzzled air,
desperately searching around for the ice cream parlour,
then screaming, "It's unfair," and rolling on the floor,
and when we were told that some centuries ago,
they chopped off the head of the king who lived there,
we all said,   "Serves him right for being such a liar."

Rowing on Lac Daumesnil

It is the Britishest of all French outings.
There's wine for the adults and juice for the kids,
and half a baguette stuffed with that smelly cheese.
            We're rowing on Lac Daumesnil.

Of all Parisian things, it's the most civilised.
The boats apologise when they bump against ducks.
The furry islands look like they've just escaped
            from English picture books.

It is the safest way to be adventurous:
some minor tragic things might happen.
An ice cream scoop might drown,
an angry swan might snap,
            maybe someone will get sunburnt.

When we get home tonight, the children will sleep well,
the adults even better, warm and tired,
and in everyone's dreams, the beds will rock a little
            to the ripples of Lac Daumesnil.

Montmartre

It's our Everest! Look at the icing-sugar basilisk
that tops it, excellent nineteenth-century taste,
it hurts your teeth
just to stare at it, as you walk up
or take the funicular. This is no place for bikes.

Too hilly! A hill once haunted by penniless painters,
writers, musicians, cold, sick and passionate, the story goes.
This is the hill of all excesses. Wine grows on one of its faces.
Under a red windmill, young legs lift
whipped-cream-like petticoats to the tune of cancan.
This is a hill so rich, so poor. So touristy,

and yet so Paris-that-tourists-don't-want-to-see.
The history of fights for freedom,
of the workers and artists who stared at the city
unrolling at their feet like a golden carpet.
It must have felt good to look down, for once,
at the rich neighbours below them.

And if your legs hurt to climb it, breathe deeply —

                    see?   Somehow,
                    the air feels freer here.

Night on the Seine

Night-time on the Seine on a summer Saturday,
warm clouds cuddle the moon, the water breathes out
all of today's sun, and tinny tunes
unspool from speakers like ribbons from bobbins.

I walk among the spinning dancers. Feels like they spring
from nowhere every year, sprinkled there by summer.
They never stop smiling; it seems so simple to dance
on the banks of the Seine on a Saturday night.

Sometimes a boat roars past and drenches
us all in light. Crayons the bridges in white.
Shadows of dancers splatter against the walls
scratched by graffiti. Then the night shuffles back

into place. And a smile dances back on my face.

Métro Line 6,
Bir-Hakeim to Passy

It's a Sunday night. Nobody likes Sunday nights;
Sunday nights taste of the weekend ending,
of homework you haven't finished doing.
Sunday blues. You swing bluely to the beat of the metro,
windows dark-blue reflect your face thinking
of homework left to do —   but then —
wait for it — it's very sudden,
not very long — only between Bir-Hakeim and Passy —
one suspended moment, when suddenly
we   all   take   off!   We   are
not in a tunnel any more, this is
not a Sunday night any more, we're flying!
Windows no longer dark, but showing
the Eiffel Tower, there! To the right!
Hello, yellow tower in the dark surprise of night! And at its feet,
all the lights of a city that doesn't want it to be Sunday night!
It's just a flash, everyone watches, a stretch   of bright,   so brief.

Between Bir-Hakeim and Passy on Line 6 of the Paris Métro,
lift your head, and you'll see it too,
one Sunday night, when you're feeling blue,
when nothing's right, and there's school tomorrow,
and homework left to do.

Paris Snapshots

The bustling streets of Paris are known all over the world for their rich history, art and culture. In fact, Paris boasts over 6,000 streets (known as *rues*). From tree-lined boulevards and historic coffee houses to iconic art galleries and night-time viewpoints, there's always something new to discover on the streets of the City of Light. So, the next time you visit or dream about Paris, remember that every corner holds a piece of history waiting to be uncovered!

Notre-Dame

Notre-Dame is a medieval Gothic cathedral with a towering spire, stone carvings and beautiful stained-glass windows.

Fun fact: Victor Hugo's novel *The Hunchback of Notre-Dame*, published in 1831, was so popular that it saved the building from demolition.

Did you know? The main bell in Notre-Dame is called Emmanuel and it weighs over 13,000 kilograms — that's heavier than 30 grand pianos.

The Eiffel Tower

With its dazzling light shows and iconic silhouette, the Eiffel Tower welcomes thousands of visitors every day.

Fun fact: Gustave Eiffel, one of the engineers, built an apartment at the top of the tower where he hosted famous guests like Thomas Edison.

Did you know? The Eiffel Tower was originally supposed to be temporary — it was built for the 1889 World's Fair and it was planned to be taken down 20 years later. Over time it became an iconic symbol of Paris so it was never demolished.

Paris Cafés

Centuries ago, famous artists, writers and philosophers used to gather in Paris cafés to share their ideas with each other.

Fun fact: There are around 1,600 cafés in Paris; the first to call itself a café was *Le Procope*, founded in 1686.

Did you know? The first screening of a film with moving pictures took place in the Grand Café in Paris. The screening, made by the French brothers Auguste and Louis Lumière, featured 10 films, each lasting about 50 seconds.

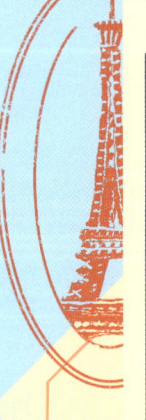

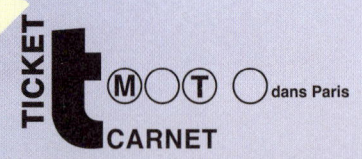
TICKET t M T O dans Paris CARNET

The River Seine

Paris started out as a small island on the Seine. Since then, the river has seen thousands of years of life and history.

Fun fact: In the nineteenth century, people took their dogs to the Seine to be bathed and groomed.

Did you know? Every year in the summer, roads along the riverbanks are covered in sand and palm trees, turning them into temporary beaches, called Paris-Plages.

♥ PARIS

The Louvre

The Louvre is Paris's national museum and art gallery, and is home to over 380,000 extraordinary paintings from around the world.

Fun fact: The Louvre is the world's largest museum — at 73,000 square metres, it's larger than 10 football pitches!

Did you know? The Mona Lisa, painted by Leonardo da Vinci, is located at the Louvre. It is the world's most famous painting. Around 10 million people visit the museum every year; 80 per cent of them are only there to see the Mona Lisa.

Once home to French kings, the Palace of Versailles attracts visitors today for its impressive art and architecture.

Fun fact: The palace is so large that King Louis XV often ate his meals cold, as the kitchen was so far from the dining room!

Did you know? Every year, the Palace of Versailles hosts a masquerade ball where guests dress and dance in Baroque costumes.

Palace of Versailles

BAGGAGE TAG

INTERNATIONAL AIRW

PARIS

PA

WE

DATE:

FLIGHT: